Masterful Images
THE ART OF KIYOSHI SAITO

Barry Till

Pomegranate
PORTLAND • OREGON

Published by Pomegranate Communications, Inc.
19018 NE Portal Way, Portland, OR 97230
800 227 1428 | www.pomegranate.com

Pomegranate Europe Ltd.
Unit 1, Heathcote Business Centre, Hurlbutt Road
Warwick, Warwickshire CV34 6TD, UK
[+44] 0 1926 430111 | sales@pomeurope.co.uk

To learn about new releases and special offers from Pomegranate, please visit www.pomegranate.com
and sign up for our e-mail newsletter. For all other queries, see "Contact Us" on our home page.

© 2013 Yoshino Watanabe
Images courtesy the Art Gallery of Greater Victoria

The contents of this book are protected by copyright, including all images and all text. This copyrighted material may not be reproduced or transmitted in any form or by any means, electronic or mechanical, including but not limited to photocopying, scanning, recording, or by any information storage or retrieval system, without the express permission in writing of the copyright holders. All rights to the images and text are reserved.

Unless otherwise stated, the artworks in this book are woodblock prints or collagraphs (i.e., woodblock prints with a design built up with textured materials creating a relief).

FRONT COVER: *Garden, Autumn, Aizu*, 1972. Fred and Isabel Pollard Collection, AGGV 1973.137.001
BACK COVER: Kiyoshi Saito, 1953

Library of Congress Cataloging-in-Publication Data
Till, Barry, 1951–
Masterful images : the art of Kiyoshi Saito / Barry Till.
pages cm
"In 1990 the Art Gallery of Greater Victoria published an exhibition catalogue entitled Woodblock Prints by Kiyoshi Saito with an essay by Barry Till. The present publication is in part based on that previous publication, which is now out of print."
Includes bibliographical references.
ISBN 978-0-7649-6455-8 (hardcover)
1. Saito, Kiyoshi, 1907-1997—Criticism and interpretation. 2. Sosaku hanga. I. Title.
NE1325.S3T55 2013
769.92—dc23
2012037947
Pomegranate Catalog No. A218
Designed by Gina Bostian

Printed in China
22 21 20 19 18 17 16 15 14 13 10 9 8 7 6 5 4 3 2 1

THE PRINTS

Snow and Sunset, 1975
Gift of Ron Longstaffe, AGGV 1995.041.001

Masterful Images

THE ART OF KIYOSHI SAITO

KIYOSHI SAITO (1907–1997) was one of the grand masters of the twentieth-century Japanese print movement known as *sosaku hanga,* meaning "original creative print." The term was coined to distinguish this new work from the traditional Japanese prints known as *ukiyo-e* and the more recent *shin hanga* (new prints), both of which relied on the *hanmoto* system, a collaboration among the artist, the block carver, the printer, and the publisher. Saito and his fellow *sosaku hanga* artists believed that just one person should make the original design, carve the woodblock, and draw the print—*jiga* 自画, *jikoku* 自刻, *jizuri* 自刷. This meant the artist was the sole creator from start to finish, motivated entirely by a desire for self-expression and art for art's sake.

Saito was the first *sosaku hanga* printmaker to become very popular in the West and is credited with a large share of the success in making modern Japanese prints popular the world over.

Early Life

Kiyoshi Saito was born on April 27, 1907, in Aizubange, a small village in Fukushima prefecture, on Honshu, Japan's central island. Because his father lost his business, the family moved to the northern island of Hokkaido, where his father worked in the coal mines of Otaru. Saito was five at the time and would suffer many hardships as he grew up in poverty. When he was thirteen years old, his mother died and Saito was sent off to become a custodian at a Buddhist temple. He hated the spartan lifestyle, tried to run away, and was eventually allowed to return home.

In order to support himself, Saito took up a sign-painting apprenticeship; before turning twenty he set up his own business designing signs for storefronts. However, his dreams of becoming an artist drove him, around 1932, to give up his business in favor of studying art in Tokyo. At the Hongo Painting

Institute, Saito studied Western-style painting, producing some oil paintings for exhibitions. Frustrated that these works did not win the recognition he had hoped for, he began experimenting, making prints from a single block that he carved himself. Saito never found a satisfactory teacher, so he ended up teaching himself the techniques of printing. As a result, his methods were quite unusual. He started out making only one copy of each work but soon realized that he could produce many copies. During this phase of experimenting with woodblock printing, he also continued working in oils.

Recognition

Saito exhibited a number of works with the Japanese Woodblock Association (Nihon Hanga Kyokai) in 1936 and at that time began to consider printmaking his main art form. He joined the Plastic Print Association (Zokei Hanga Kyokai) in 1937 at the urging of another great *sosaku hanga* artist, Tadashige Ono (1909–1990). The group showed him the possibilities of using several plates to produce multicolor woodblock prints; this encounter launched Saito in the direction of his distinctive personal style.

That same year he began to draw on the landscape of Aizu, the area where he had grown up, as a subject in his prints. The theme of snowy rural Japan would become his trademark, and time and again he would return to this subject matter throughout his long and illustrious career.[1] It was in 1942, during World War II, that he first exhibited his Aizu prints in a small gallery above a brush and paper store.

From 1943 or 1944 until 1954 Saito was employed by the Asahi Newspaper Company. While working there he met with the legendary Shiko Munakata (1903–1975) and the early *sosaku hanga* pioneer artist Koshiro Onchi (1891–1955). Onchi had founded the First Thursday Society (Ichimokukai) in 1939 and became something of a mentor for Saito. The society, which included future *sosaku hanga* printmakers like Gen Yamaguchi (1896–1976) and Jun'ichiro Sekino (1914–1988), provided aspiring young artists with resources and comradeship during the war years when materials were scarce and censorship was severe. Members met once a month to circulate and discuss their prints. In the years following the armistice, this group would prove crucial to the *sosaku hanga* movement.

In 1947, when a new Tokyo gallery across from Frank Lloyd Wright's Imperial Hotel showed Saito's prints alongside the work of Un'ichi Hiratsuka (1895–1997) and Hide Kawanishi (1894–1965), Saito sold his first print. The following year he participated in the Salon Printemps, an American-sponsored exhibition benefiting Japanese artists. Servicemen and their wives, American connoisseurs and tourists soon discovered Saito, and they were instrumental in launching his meteoric career. During the years following Japan's surrender, Saito found himself inundated with orders from foreign collectors that he could barely fill. This newfound recognition allowed him to become a full-time artist. Soon his work was being displayed in important exhibitions and purchased by renowned galleries, museums, and important collectors. News magazines commissioned illustrations, and commercial enterprises hired him to produce graphic designs.

Despite this breakthrough, he had been largely ignored by his countrymen until 1951, when a print entitled *Steady Gaze* was shown at the first biennial exhibition sponsored by the São Paulo Museum of Modern Art in Brazil and won first prize, beating out entries in all other media. Tetsuro Komai (1920–1976), a Japanese etcher, was also honored. The triumph of prints over oil paintings and sculptures shocked Japan's art world, which had traditionally maintained a condescending attitude toward prints. This international attention assured the survival and development of Japan's modern print movement. An international competition held in Ljubljana, Slovenia, in 1956 also brought a prize; a solo exhibition followed, at the Corcoran Gallery of Art in Washington, DC. The same year, one of Saito's prints appeared on the cover of the first major book in English on the *sosaku hanga* movement: Oliver Statler's *Modern Japanese Prints: An Art Reborn* (1956); Saito was one of a small number of artists to be profiled. Invited by the Department of State and the Asia Foundation, he made a trip to the United States in 1956. Fortunate students attended the printmaking courses he taught in Ann Arbor, Michigan, and visited the exhibition "Woodcuts by Kiyoshi Saito," held at the University of Michigan Museum of Art from April 17 to 23, 1956. Recognized as a master, Saito exhibited widely in both the United States and Europe. In 1967 he was even asked to make a print of Prime Minister Eisaku Sato for the cover of *Time* magazine.

Oeuvre

In the years following the São Paulo award, Saito's art became enormously popular both at home and abroad. His prints remained remarkably innovative over the next several decades, but his unique style is almost always immediately recognizable.

Kiyoshi Saito creating a portrait of Prime Minister Eisaku Sato at his official residence, 1967

Saito stated that his strongest influences were not Japanese artists but European painters like Piet Mondrian, Pablo Picasso, Henri Matisse, Wassily Kandinsky, Paul Gauguin, Odilon Redon, and Edvard Munch—their romanticism, exoticism, mysticism, and minimalism cast a spell on the young artist. He particularly appreciated the use Munch and Gauguin made of wood grain and the orderly beauty and simple architecture displayed in works by Mondrian. Asked about Japan's classical *ukiyo-e* prints of the eighteenth and nineteenth centuries, Saito frankly declared that he had at first found them "nauseating." However, after he realized that *ukiyo-e* prints had exerted an enormous influence on his favorite Western artists, he began to reassess his opinion of them. He once commented: "It was only through Gauguin that I began to appreciate the qualities of *ukiyo-e,* but I still feel closer to Gauguin than to *ukiyo-e.*"[2] Like Van Gogh and Gauguin, Saito came to be influenced by the *ukiyo-e* artists. Like them, he adopted a vertical format, truncated his central subjects, divided his compositions into simple geometric zones filled out with solid areas of color and large empty spaces, and adopted a high or low viewpoint to collapse foreground and background into the same plane.

Perhaps Munch's focus on his native place influenced Saito. With simplicity and vigor, he conveyed in every print of Aizu his nostalgic respect for this remote mountainous area. The images capture the seasons and times of day, evoking the different moods that accompany the changing colors and temperatures. A deep awareness of the locale enabled the artist to reveal, with fine sensitivity, both the sorrows and the joys of rural life. At times, simple shapes convey strong emotions. In particular, his scenes with a single figure in a landscape create a lonely, somber mood. Late in his career, Saito liked to sketch panoramic views reminiscent of ancient Japanese horizontal handscrolls, some of which extended to a length of twenty feet. He then would cut the scene into smaller sections to produce individual prints.

The prints cover many topics: animals such as chickens, cattle, cats, and dogs; human beings, including Saito's only child, Naoko; *maiko* (geishas in training) and bunraku puppeteers; ancient works of art such as Buddhist statues, *haniwa* clay funerary figurines, and Jomon-period figures and pottery; flowers and vegetables; the Buddhist temples, Shinto shrines, and rock gardens of Kyoto, Nara, and Kamakura—the ancient capitals; and themes drawn from travel to India, Tahiti, Indonesia, France, Mexico, and the United States. Still, Saito's favorite subject remained the Japanese landscape, particularly his childhood village, Aizu. When he endowed scenes otherwise quiet and restful with a mysterious perspective rich in complex patterns and pathways, the artist created intriguing juxtapositions, suggesting the deep bonds between people and their natural or built surroundings.

Flat areas of color and the texture of the woodblocks' grain communicate the essentials of nature in bold and harmonious designs. Saito's simple style possesses great freedom and spontaneity, and there is an intentional avoidance of elegant refinement. Clearly defined visual

Haniwa (3), n.d.
Gift of Ron Longstaffe, AGGV 1995.041.004

Deep Winter in Aizu, 1958
Fred and Isabel Pollard Collection, AGGV 1969.084.001

Kiyoshi Saito in Aizu, 1984

elements and areas of rich-textured earthy colors blend well with the realistic subject matter. Sure execution and expression reveal a confident artist. The prints of ancient sculptures have a classic grace, and the Buddhist images are filled with compassion and serenity. Some of the slender figures are wrapped in a veil of spiritual mysticism.

Saito's depictions of animals—he was especially fond of cats—are deliberately unsophisticated and primitive, yet their visual impact is stunning. One of his most brilliant prints, created in 1973, is a rough-hewn image called *Suspicious Eyes* (p. 109). To capture the texture of fur, he exploited the natural patterns present in his woodblock—a technique referred to as *mokumezuri* or "wood-grain printing"—achieving a dynamic graphic effect.

At the outset of his printmaking career, Saito used solid blocks of *katsura* (*Cercidiphyllum japonicum*) wood from Hokkaido. However, as time went on *katsura* became more and more difficult to acquire, so he switched to using plywood faced with various Japanese woods, like rowan (mountain ash, genus *Sorbus*), *yanagi* (willow, genus *Salix*), *keyaki* (*Zelkova serrata*), *shina* (*Tilia japonica*), and *lauan* (*Shorea teysmanniana*). These ensured a wide range of patterns and textures. *Keyaki* was a great favorite, as it had the broad longitudinal grain that suited his designs.

Because Saito taught himself the technique of printmaking, his color prints are dramatically individual. He developed an unusual and distinct method of making a print from a single block, which he cut freehand using a *kiri* (a Japanese carpenter's tool) to dig out or scratch at the wood. Using this process, he could print only a single color at a time. His print block had no registration guidelines, so he set weights along the borders of his paper to keep it from moving until each color dried. This process was laborious: up to half a day might be needed to produce just one print. He later tried another technique, using as many as five or six different plywood blocks, one for each color. This allowed him to make many more prints in the same print run. After applying the first color and letting it dry, he proceeded to the next carved block, using registration marks to apply the second color, and so on. This allowed him to make a relatively large number of prints. On other occasions he used lithography methods and painted directly onto the block before drawing a print.

For paper he preferred the long-fibered Echizen *hosho* (mulberry paper) from Fukui prefecture, a particularly absorbent and flexible choice. His tints were a combination of dark *sumi* ink, made from soot derived from pine branches, and water-based colors. Having inked his block, Saito set a sheet of *hosho* atop it then used the traditional *baren* (a circular pad, usually made of a bamboo sheath wrapped around a flat coil of straw or bamboo fiber that has been reinforced by a multilayered paper disk) to burnish the back of the paper. The result, after several passes, was typically a composition in earthy hues of grey, beige, black, and white, with delicate shading.

In addition to woodblock prints, Saito also produced oil paintings and color-and-ink paintings (*suiboku ga*). He also made prints using drypoint and collagraphy.[3] The latter

Tosyodai-ji, Nara, 1959
Fred and Isabel Pollard Collection
AGGV 1974.104.001

involves pulling proofs from a rigid matrix on which a sort of collage is built up with textured materials, creating a relief.

In 1981 Kiyoshi Saito was awarded the Order of the Sacred Treasure, the highest civil honor issued by the Japanese state. The Order of Culture followed, in 1995.[4] The prize commitees praised the artist's lifelong commitment to promoting Japanese modern prints around the world and to teaching the printmaking process.[5] He continued practicing his craft until he passed away at age ninety on November 14, 1997, just after a major retrospective exhibit had been held at the Wako Department Store, one of Tokyo's long-established and prestigious galleries in the heart of the Ginza district.

Legacy

Saito combined Japanese aesthetic elements with cubist, modernist, abstract, and impressionist qualities, achieving a rare synthesis of East and West and of old and new. His poetic works have remained timeless; in spite of their foreign influences, they remain uniquely and unmistakably Japanese. The viewer is constantly challenged by Saito's formal inventiveness. His prints display a remarkable integrity, and they will undoubtedly continue to be admired the world over for many years to come.[6]

Throughout his lifetime, Saito generously donated prints and blocks to various American museums, including the Art Institute of Chicago, the Museum of Fine Arts in Boston, and the University of Michigan Museum of Art in Ann Arbor. He also gave a large number of woodblock prints, collagraphs, and sketches that cover his entire career to a museum in Fukushima City, which opened just before his death. Apparently, one of the provisions of his gift was that the work be made available to any American or European museum that sent a request. The Yanaizu Municipal Saito Kiyoshi Museum was set up in the Kawanuma district of Fukushima to house this collection of about 850 of his works of art.[7] The museum holds four special exhibitions a year with about ninety prints on display on each occasion.

To this day, Saito's artworks are highly sought after and can be found in major public and private collections around the world.[8]

Kiyoshi Saito with his print *Jealousy*, 1953

Notes

1. Snow scenes in Aizu were among Saito's favorite subjects. In a letter to me dated September 7, 1990, he wrote, "I have made eighty-four prints of 'winter in Aizu' and hope to live some years more to make the hundredth one."
2. Oliver Statler and Chisaburoh F. Yamada, *Kiyoshi Saito* (Tokyo: Kodansha, 1957), 1.
3. "The word collagraph, which derives from 'collage' and 'graphic,' was coined by a Seattle artist, Glen Alps, who is credited with developing the technique in the mid 1950s. Saito had learned about collagraphs during a visit to Seattle in 1982 and was intrigued by the textural effects that could be achieved with them." See Donald Jenkins, *"Winter in Aizu" and Other Prints by Kiyoshi Saito* (Portland, OR: Portland Art Museum, 1988), 3.
4. The Order of the Sacred Treasure (*zuiho sho*) was established on January 4, 1888, by the Meiji emperor. It is awarded to those who have made distinguished contributions to various fields, including the arts. The Order of Culture (*bunka kunsho*) was established on February 11, 1937. Conferred by the emperor in person on Culture Day (November 3) each year, the award goes to those who have made significant contributions to Japanese culture; the recipients receive an allowance for the rest of their lives.
5. Kiyoshi Saito had an assistant named Kazuyuki Ohtsu (born 1935) who worked with him for four decades until Saito's death in 1997. Ohtsu is a woodblock print artist in his own right and has widely exhibited his work.
6. Oliver Statler feels that the word *integrity* best describes Saito's work. Statler once wrote, "Through all of [Kiyoshi Saito's] work runs a search for fundamentals, a closeness to the earth and its strength. There is a respect in his work, too; respect for his medium, and respect for his subject matter. These are qualities which are important, and that is the reason for their wide appeal. We each of us feel their need, and we are grateful to Saito for expressing them." See Statler and Yamada, *Kiyoshi Saito*, 3.
7. This is the same Fukushima that suffered the effects of the devastating east Japan earthquake in 2011, the tsunami that followed, and the resulting Fukushima I Nuclear Power Plant disaster. The museum is not located in the evacuation zone.
8. According to information on the Internet, some of the public collections that own works by Kiyoshi Saito include the Achenbach Foundation for Graphic Arts, San Francisco; the Art Gallery of New South Wales, Sydney; the Art Institute of Chicago; the British Museum, London; the Cincinnati Art Museum; the Currier Museum of Art, Manchester, New Hampshire; the Dallas Museum of Art; the Fukushima Prefectural Museum of Art; the Harvard Art Museums, Cambridge, Massachusetts; the Indianapolis Museum of Art; the Kanagawa Prefectural Museum of Cultural History; the Los Angeles County Museum of Art; the Metropolitan Museum of Art, New York; the Miami Art Museum; the Mississippi Museum of Art, Jackson; the Museum of Fine Arts, Boston; the Museum of Modern Art, New York; the National Museum of Modern Art, Tokyo; and the Pacific Asia Museum, Pasadena.

Aizu

Winter in Aizu, 1938
Fred and Isabel Pollard Collection, AGGV 1966.022.001

Winter in Aizu, 1938
Fred and Isabel Pollard Collection, AGGV 1966.023.001

Winter in Aizu, 1938
Fred and Isabel Pollard Collection, AGGV 1966.076.001

Winter in Aizu, 1953
Fred and Isabel Pollard Collection, AGGV 1967.057.001

Winter in Aizu, 1953
Fred and Isabel Pollard Collection, AGGV 1967.058.001

Winter in Aizu, 1958
Fred and Isabel Pollard Collection, AGGV 1967.033.001

Winter in Aizu, 1958
Fred and Isabel Pollard Collection, AGGV 1964.156.001

Winter in Aizu, 1958
Fred and Isabel Pollard Collection, AGGV 1966.079.001

Winter in Aizu, 1958
Fred and Isabel Pollard Collection, AGGV 1967.034.001

Winter in Aizu, 1958
Fred and Isabel Pollard Collection, AGGV 1966.038.001

Aizu Yanaizu, Fukushima, 1965
Fred and Isabel Pollard Collection, AGGV 1967.160.001

Winter in Aizu, n.d.
Fred and Isabel Pollard Collection, AGGV 1967.038.001

Children of Aizu, n.d.
Fred and Isabel Pollard Collection, AGGV 1962.007.001

Winter in Aizu, n.d.
Fred and Isabel Pollard Collection, AGGV 1969.101.001

Winter in Aizu, 1967
Fred and Isabel Pollard Collection, AGGV 1968.145.001

Snow, Aizu, n.d.
Fred and Isabel Pollard Collection, AGGV 1962.006.001

Winter in Tsuruga-jyo, Aizu Wakamatsu, 1967
Fred and Isabel Pollard Collection, AGGV 1968.149.001

Winter in Aizu, 1969
Fred and Isabel Pollard Collection, AGGV 1970.138.00

Winter in Aizu, 1969
Fred and Isabel Pollard Collection, AGGV 1969.102.001

Garden, Autumn, Aizu, 1972
Fred and Isabel Pollard Collection, AGGV 1973.137.001

May in Aizu, 1988
Harold and Vera Mortimer Lamb Purchase Fund, AGGV 1991.013.001

Temples and Gardens Kyoto and Nara

Ancient City, Nara, 1954
Fred and Isabel Pollard Collection, AGGV 1966.080.001

Gate, Horyu-ji, Nara (B), 1970
Fred and Isabel Pollard Collection, AGGV 1970.136.001

Nanzen-ji, Kyoto, 1963
Fred and Isabel Pollard Collection, AGGV 1967.168.001

Katsura, Kyoto (D), 1958
Gift of Ron Longstaffe, AGGV 1995.041.002

Kozan-ji Temple, Kyoto, 1974
Fred and Isabel Pollard Collection
AGGV 1975.006.001

Autumn in Kyoto, 1969
Fred and Isabel Pollard Collection, AGGV 1970.010.001

Shisen-do, Kyoto, 1971
Fred and Isabel Pollard Collection, AGGV 1973.138.001

Miyoshin-ji, Kyoto, 1965
Fred and Isabel Pollard Collection, AGGV 1968.119.001

Kozan-ji, Kyoto, 1965
Fred and Isabel Pollard Collection
AGGV 1967.205.001

Katsura, Kyoto, 1955
Fred and Isabel Pollard Collection, AGGV 1962.111.001

Garden, Sendogosyo, Kyoto, 1958
Fred and Isabel Pollard Collection, AGGV 1966.036.001

Katsura, Kyoto, 1970
Fred and Isabel Pollard Collection, AGGV 1971.005.001

Katsura, Kyoto, 1970
Fred and Isabel Pollard Collection, AGGV 1970.135.001

Stone Garden, Ryoan-ji, 1955
Fred and Isabel Pollard Collection, AGGV 1968.263.001

Stone Garden, Kyoto (C), 1965
Fred and Isabel Pollard Collection
AGGV 1967.030.001

Katsura, Kyoto, 1970
Fred and Isabel Pollard Collection, AGGV 1970.131.001

Buddha Asyura, Nara (C), 1959
Gift of Roy G. Cole, AGGV 1992.051.031

Asuka, n.d.
Fred and Isabel Pollard Collection
AGGV 1967.176.001

Buddha Miroku, 1957
Fred and Isabel Pollard Collection
AGGV 1966.051.001

Buddha Asyura, Nara, 1959
Fred and Isabel Pollard Collection, AGGV 1968.136.001

Head of Kwannon, n.d.
Fred and Isabel Pollard Collection
AGGV 1972.236.001

Dream (B), 1971
Fred and Isabel Pollard Collection, AGGV 1973.129.001

Buddha Siamese, 1957
Gift of Roy G. Cole, AGGV 1992.051.133

Other Locations

Otaru, Hokkaido, 1948
Fred and Isabel Pollard Collection, AGGV 1980.019.001

Sheds, n.d.
Fred and Isabel Pollard Collection, AGGV 1967.054.001

Bell Tower, 1958
Gift of Ron Longstaffe, AGGV 1995.041.003

Hirato, Nagasaki, 1965
Fred and Isabel Pollard Collection, AGGV 1966.091.001

Nikko, 1969
Fred and Isabel Pollard Collection, AGGV 1970.137.001

Village of Mito, n.d.
Fred and Isabel Pollard Collection, AGGV 1962.005.001

Ploughing the Rice Field, n.d.
Fred and Isabel Pollard Collection, AGGV 1973.124.001

Gate, Kamakura, 1972
Fred and Isabel Pollard Collection, AGGV 1973.126.001

Farm House Scene, 1975
Gift of Ron Longstaffe, AGGV 1995.041.007

Foreign Lands

Girl Smelling Flowers (Tahiti), n.d.
Fred and Isabel Pollard Collection, AGGV 1967.017.001

Girl in Autumn (Tahiti), 1952
Fred and Isabel Pollard Collection, AGGV 1967.023.001

Design in Red and Black (Wayang Puppet from Java), n.d.
Fred and Isabel Pollard Collection, AGGV 1967.053.001

Country (Mexico), 1956
Fred and Isabel Pollard Collection, AGGV 1968.138.001

Resting (Mexico), 1956
Fred and Isabel Pollard Collection
AGGV 1968.172.001

Chapel in Paris, 1960
Fred and Isabel Pollard Collection
AGGV 1968.174.001

Winter in Paris, 1966
Fred and Isabel Pollard Collection
AGGV 1968.146.001

India, 1968
Fred and Isabel Pollard Collection, AGGV 1970.130.001

Tenderness (A), 1968
Fred and Isabel Pollard Collection, AGGV 1970.139.001

Ancient Clay

Clay Image, 1952
Fred and Isabel Pollard Collection
AGGV 1967.216.001

Clay Image, 1955
Fred and Isabel Pollard Collection
AGGV 1968.173.001

Dogu (B), 1958
Fred and Isabel Pollard Collection
AGGV 1968.169.001

Haniwa, 1969
Fred and Isabel Pollard Collection
AGGV 1971.020.001

Clay Image, 1969
Fred and Isabel Pollard Collection, AGGV 1968.222.001

Bunraku and Maiko

Maiko, Kyoto, 1961
Fred and Isabel Pollard Collection
AGGV 1969.103.001

Bunraku, n.d.
Gift of Ron Longstaffe, AGGV 1995.041.006

Bunraku (G), 1961
Fred and Isabel Pollard Collection, AGGV 1973.127.001

Maiko, Kyoto, 1960
Fred and Isabel Pollard Collection
AGGV 1967.046.001

Figures

Ecstasy (A), 1950
Fred and Isabel Pollard Collection
AGGV 1967.045.001

Nude, designed 1950, printed 1955
Fred and Isabel Pollard Collection
AGGV 1971.006.001

Knitting, 1966
Fred and Isabel Pollard Collection
AGGV 1968.152.001

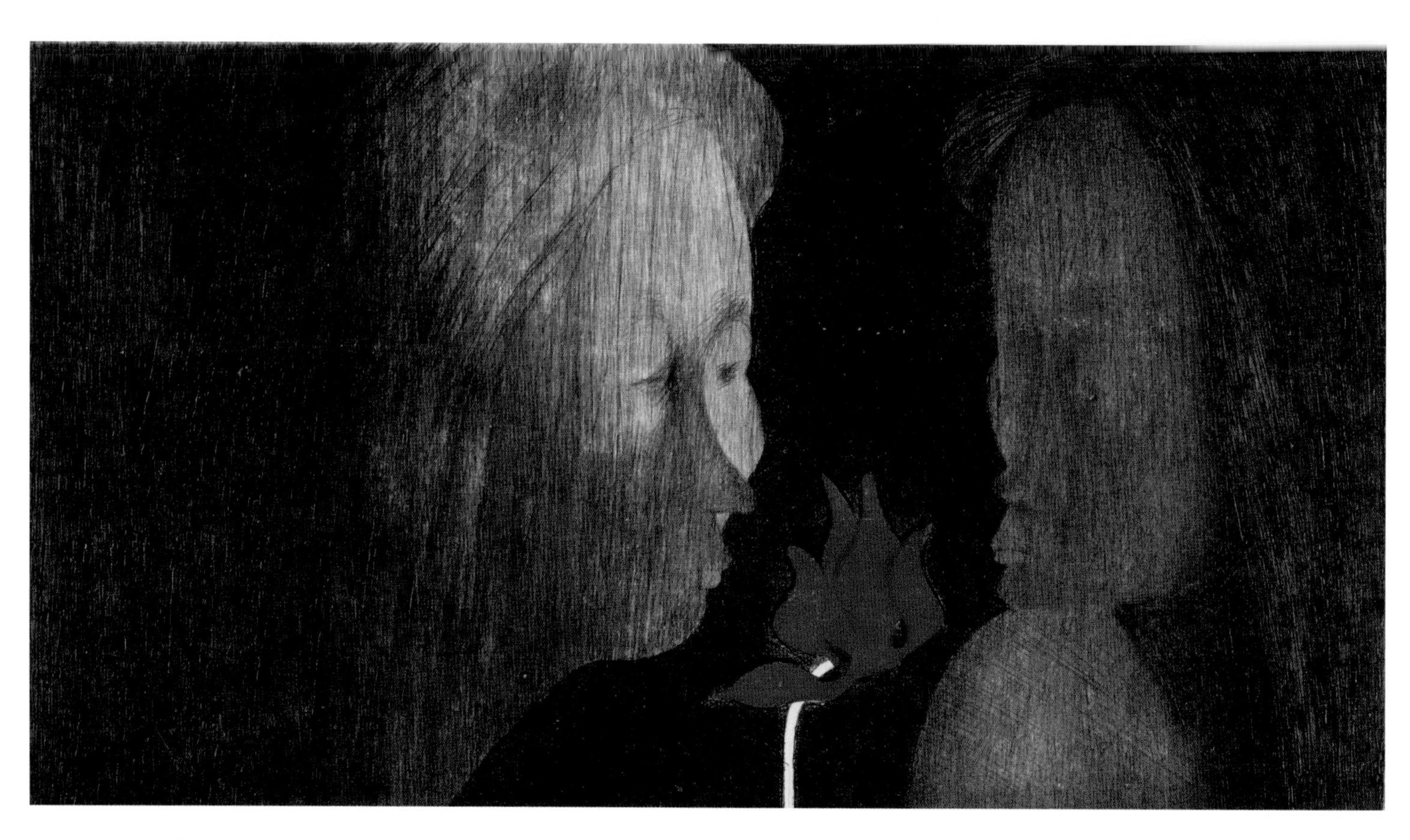

Red Flower, 1968
Drypoint
Fred and Isabel Pollard Collection, AGGV 1968.141.001

Naoko (Daughter), 1968
Drypoint
Fred and Isabel Pollard Collection
AGGV 1968.140.001

Naoko, 1966
Fred and Isabel Pollard Collection
AGGV 1968.148.001

Profile, 1948
Fred and Isabel Pollard Collection
AGGV 1973.125.001

Red Nude, c. 1960s
Oil painting
Fred and Isabel Pollard Collection
AGGV 1967.122.001

Resting, 1946
Fred and Isabel Pollard
Collection
AGGV 1973.142.001

Evening, 1961
Gift of Roy G. Cole, AGGV 1992.051.044

Pansy, 1964
Fred and Isabel Pollard Collection
AGGV 1966.081.001

Animals

Jealousy, n.d.
Fred and Isabel Pollard Collection
AGGV 1967.174.001

Mother Love, 1964
Fred and Isabel Pollard Collection
AGGV 1971.001.001

Cats and Butterfly, n.d.
Fred and Isabel Pollard Collection
AGGV 1968.045.001

Dachshund, 1955
Fred and Isabel Pollard Collection, AGGV 1967.055.001

Suspicious Eyes, 1973
Fred and Isabel Pollard Collection, AGGV 1975.007.001

Bibliography

Jenkins, Donald. *"Winter in Aizu" and Other Prints by Kiyoshi Saito*. Portland, OR: Portland Art Museum, 1988.

Merritt, Helen, and Nanako Yamada. *Guide to Modern Japanese Woodblock Prints: 1900–1975*. Honolulu: University of Hawaii Press, 1992.

Petit, Gaston, and Amadio Arboleda. *Evolving Techniques in Japanese Woodblock Prints*. Tokyo: Kodansha, 1977.

Saito Kiyoshi Museum. *Saito Kiyoshi Bijutsukan shozo sakuhinshu* (Catalogue of works in the Kiyoshi Saito Museum). Yanaizu-cho: Yanaizu Choritsu Saito Kiyoshi Bijutsukan, 1999.

Smith, Lawrence. *Modern Japanese Prints, 1912–1989.* New York: Cross River Press, 1994.

Statler, Oliver. *Modern Japanese Prints: An Art Reborn*. Rutland, VT: Tuttle, 1956.

Statler, Oliver, and Chisaburoh F. Yamada. *Kiyoshi Saito*. Tokyo: Kodansha, 1957.

Till, Barry. *Woodblock Prints by Kiyoshi Saito*. Victoria, B.C.: Art Gallery of Greater Victoria, 1990.

Acknowledgments

The Art Gallery of Greater Victoria (AGGV) in British Columbia, Canada, is indeed fortunate to have 112 prints as well as an oil painting by the prolific artist Kiyoshi Saito. To the best of our knowledge, this is the second largest public collection of his work in North America, second only to the Cleveland Museum of Art, which has about 200 works.

AGGV would like to thank the holder of the Kiyoshi Saito copyright, Yoshino Watanabe, for granting permission to produce this book on his work. It is a long overdue tribute to this man of extraordinary artistic talents.

We wish to thank Ms. Junko Preniqi of the Art Gallery of Greater Victoria for her generous help with the translation of the correspondence regarding copyright. Also, we thank Bob Matheson for the wonderful photography in this book and Lori Graves for checking the labels.

Barry Till
Curator of Asian Art
Art Gallery of Greater Victoria